Dino Tales

A collection of six stories

Written by Katiuscia Giusti

Illustrations by Agnes Lemaire, color by Doug Calder

ISBN-13: 978-3-03730-213-2

www.auroraproduction.com

Operation Oops!

Grandpa Jake heard an angry cry from Tristan's bedroom. He hurried upstairs and opened the bedroom door to see a teary-eyed boy. Tristan held his favorite fire engine. The ladder that extended from the engine's back was broken.

"Troy broke my fire engine," Tristan said, in between sobs. "He stepped on it."

"I didn't see it," Troy said sadly.

"But you broke it!" Tristan cried.

"I'm sorry," Troy said. "Maybe we can fix it." Troy felt bad for breaking the fire engine. He hadn't done it on purpose.

"Let me take a look at it," Grandpa Jake offered. "Perhaps there is something we can do to fix it."

"I don't want Troy to play with my toys any more!" Tristan said.

"Now Tristan, that's not being forgiving," said Grandpa Jake. "Troy said he was sorry, and it *was* an accident."

Tristan looked at his broken fire engine, and then at Troy. It was hard for him to forgive his friend.

"Did I ever tell you about Crispin the dinosaur?" Grandpa Jake asked.

"No," said Tristan. "Did his fire engine break too?"

"Well, no," answered Grandpa Jake, "but one day he made a mistake that made his sister unhappy. How about we take your fire engine down to the workshop, and while I try to fix it I can tell you all about Crispin?"

It had been rainy for many days. Crispin stayed inside his family's den during the storm, and kept busy planning games he could play with his friends outside once the rain stopped.

Today the sun was finally shining and Crispin hurried off to find his best friends, Wesley and Suds, to see if they wanted to play some games with him.

"Wesley!" Crispin called. "Suds! Where are you?"

Wesley poked his head out of his den. "Here I am. What's up?"

"Would you and Suds want to play some games with me?" Crispin asked. "I feel like running and playing."

"Me too," said Wesley. "Let's go find Suds."

The two friends arrived at Suds' den, and asked her if she'd like to join them.

Suds was eager to have some fun. The three friends then headed off to the nearby forest to play. They decided to play a type of "Capture the Flag," with only one flag to capture. One of the friends would hide the flag and protect it, and the other two would try to capture it.

Wesley took the first turn as protector of the flag. Suds and Crispin would have to capture it.

"One … two … three…," Crispin and Suds began counting.

Wesley hurried off with the flag to hide it. He placed it carefully inside a large, hollow tree trunk.

"Forty-nine … fifty! We're coming to capture the flag." Crispin called out loudly.

"Not if I catch you first," Wesley replied.

Crispin searched under bushes and behind boulders, but the flag was nowhere to be seen.

Suddenly he heard a playful shrill from Suds. She had found the flag, but Wesley had seen her before she had captured it, and he had run off to catch her.

Now's my chance, thought Crispin, as he ran over towards the hollow tree trunk, where he now saw the flag.

"Aha!" cried Crispin, grabbing it. "I found the flag!"

Crispin started running towards his base with the flag, but Wesley was fast and catching up quickly.

Crispin ran to the edge of the forest and into a large field.

"Ha, ha!" he shouted. "You can't catch me, Wesley!"

"Crispin! Stop!" came a loud shout.

But it was too late. Crispin had run right through his sister Dixie's flower patch. He hadn't seen it while he was running, but now many of her flowers had been trampled on and squashed by Crispin's feet.

"Uh-oh!" Wesley said with a shake of his head after seeing what Crispin had done. Suds came running out of the forest to see what had happened.

"Look what you've done, Crispin!" Dixie said. She was upset, because she had put a lot of time and care into her flower patch.

Crispin hadn't meant to ruin Dixie's flowers, and he wasn't sure what to do or say. Then he noticed there wasn't the usual fence around her garden.

"Where's your fence?" Crispin asked. "If your fence had been up, then I wouldn't have run over your flowers."

Dixie only got more upset. She angrily named the different flowers that Crispin had ruined, and talked about how much time it had taken for them to grow. Crispin argued that it was really Dixie's fault for not having her fence up.

"Wait! Wait!" cried Wesley. "It's not right to be shouting at each other. There must be some way we can work this out."

Dixie wiped her tears. "It rained so much that my little fence fell over because the ground was so muddy," Dixie explained. "That's why there was no fence."

"Well, maybe there's something we can do to help Dixie fix her garden," Suds suggested.

"Like what?" Dixie asked. "These flowers are ruined!".

10

"We could help you put your little fence back up, so that this won't happen again," Wesley said.

"And tie the flowers that are bent to little sticks, so that they'll stand upright," added Crispin.

"That's not going to work," Dixie said sadly. "I'm going to have to dig them all up and plant new flowers. I'm still angry at you, Crispin!"

"I know you're upset," Suds said. "But it was an accident, and Crispin is sorry. Will you forgive him? We can all work together to try to fix it. I'm sure some of the flowers can be saved."

"You're right, Suds," Dixie said. "I'm sorry for being so angry at you, Crispin. I forgive you, and I'd be happy to have your help to fix my garden."

Crispin smiled at his sister. "Thank you for forgiving me, Dixie. You take such good care of your flower patch, and I'm sorry about the mess I made. I can start by putting the fence back up for you, if you'd like."

"Thank you," said Dixie. "That's very nice of you, and I think some of these flowers will be okay if I give them a little extra care."

Crispin went off to find the tools he needed to help Dixie.

Suds and Wesley offered to give a hand too. Before long, Dixie's flower patch was looking beautiful again.

Crispin made a nice sign to go on the fence that read, "Caution: Flower Bed Ahead." He also brought his sister some new bulbs and seeds to plant in her garden. Dixie was so happy!

"Troy, I forgive you for accidentally breaking my fire engine," Tristan said. "I'm sorry I was angry at you. Please forgive me. I should've put my fire engine back on the shelf instead of leaving it on the floor."

"I'm sorry I broke it, and I'll try to be more careful next time," Troy replied. "Maybe I can lend you my fire engine while yours is getting fixed."

"Thank you, Troy. I'd really like that!"

"Well, boys," Grandpa Jake said, "I think this fire engine will be okay. Once the glue has dried, it will be almost like new."

"Thank you very much, Grandpa!" exclaimed Tristan. "You did such a good job of fixing it."

Moral:

Everyone makes mistakes, and needs forgiveness. Forgiveness *is* love.

My Oh My, Milton!

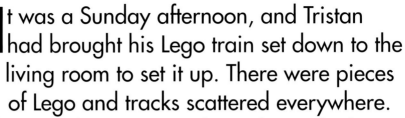

It was a Sunday afternoon, and Tristan had brought his Lego train set down to the living room to set it up. There were pieces of Lego and tracks scattered everywhere.

"Oh my!" Grandpa Jake said when he saw the mess and tiptoed his way around the many pieces. "I was upstairs looking for you."

"I came to play down here," explained Tristan. "There was no place to play in my room."

"I can understand why," said Grandpa Jake. "Your room is so messy that I could hardly open the door!"

"Mom will clean it up later," said Tristan. "I think she likes to clean up."

"Actually, Tristan, picking up after you can sometimes be a lot of work for your mother," Grandpa Jake said. "Did you know that learning to clean up after yourself and being responsible is part of growing up?"

Tristan shook his head and sighed. "I don't like to clean up. It takes me so long!"

"That's why you need to learn to pick up after yourself little by little, instead of waiting until it's

a big mess and then cleaning up. Otherwise it will be a bigger job and take longer."

"But why is it important to clean up, Grandpa?" Tristan asked.

"That's a very good question. I have a story that will help you understand the importance of being tidy and responsible."

Tristan scrambled onto the couch, ready for the story.

"Well, maybe you'd better clean up all the Lego first," Grandpa Jake suggested.

"I'll do that right away," agreed Tristan. "Then can you tell me the story?"

"It's a deal," Grandpa Jake replied.

Mr. Nuggin arrived at school carrying a large box. "Good morning, class," he said, as he placed the box on his desk.

"Good morning, Mr. Nuggin," chorused the class.

"I hope you all had a good weekend."

"Yes, we did," all the dinosaurs said as they nodded their heads.

"Excuse me, but what's in your box, Mr. Nuggin?" Dixie asked.

"Ah! Well, this morning I have a surprise. This week we will focus on learning responsibility, having good manners, and being neat and tidy. I have given each of your parents a chart to fill out this week. Every time you are responsible in your jobs, have good manners, and stay neat and tidy, they will mark it on the chart. At the end of the week, the three dinosaurs who have the best marks will each get a prize."

Mr. Nuggin opened the box and pulled out a bag that contained a small igloo tent. He then pulled out a painting kit complete with a stand and mixing palette. The third item was a set to build a small pull-wagon.

Milton's eyes lit up when he saw the wagon. He had always wanted a wagon.

School went on, but Milton could not stop thinking about the wagon. He was so interested in the prize that he hadn't paid much attention to what Mr. Nuggin had said they were to do in order to win it.

As Milton walked home from school, lost in thought about the wagon, he didn't

realize that he was walking through huge puddles of mud. By the time he got home, his shoes and pants were covered in thick, hard mud.

"Oh dear, Milton, what have you done?" his mother asked, when he arrived at his family's den.

"It's just mud, Mother," he said. "I'll change later."

"But what about the chart Mr. Nuggin made? I can't give you a good mark for not cleaning up right away when you're so dirty."

"Okay," Milton said with a sigh. He quickly changed his pants, but he didn't wipe his shoes well enough, so he left muddy footprints all over the floor of the den.

Later that evening his father came home. "Hello," he called out.

"Hello, dear," Milton's mother answered. But Milton didn't greet his dad; he was too busy playing with his toys.

Milton's father went to sit in his favorite chair, but as soon as he sat down, he let out a loud shout. "Owwwww!"

"What's the matter, dear?" Milton's mother asked.

"There's something in the chair," Milton's father answered.

In the chair were several of Milton's jacks, which he hadn't put away after playing with them.

Milton's mother shook her head sadly.

The week went on, and Milton couldn't seem to keep his clothes clean. He had driven his toy trucks in the mud, and hadn't cleaned them off, so now the wheels didn't turn because the mud had hardened on the wheels. Milton's room was a mess, his toys were scattered everywhere, and he wasn't diligent in his jobs.

"My oh my, Milton!" Mr. Nuggin exclaimed, when Milton arrived at school the following week.

Milton was a mess. On his way to school he had chased a butterfly, and in the process had ripped his pants on a fence. He ran through a puddle, getting his clothes wet, and he was late for school.

By the time Milton arrived at school, Mr. Nuggin had already passed out the prizes. Wesley had gotten the igloo tent, Suds the painting kit, and Bumble the wagon.

Milton looked down sadly, and that was when he noticed how dirty his clothes were. "I'm sorry, Mr. Nuggin. I really wanted the wagon,

but I guess I need to learn more about tidiness and good manners."

Milton went home from school feeling a little sad.

"I didn't win a prize at school today," Milton explained, when his mother asked what the matter was.

"Well, Milton, I wasn't able to put any good marks on your chart," his mother said. "I was trying to encourage you to pick up after yourself, but you didn't pay attention."

"But, Mother, it's so hard to be clean and neat!" Milton said.

"It is difficult, I know, but it's part of growing up, and it does get easier the more you do it," Milton's mother said. "We can also pray together and ask God to help you be more responsible, and to have better manners."

"I have an idea! Why don't we try again on the chart Mr. Nuggin made? We can try it for a few weeks and see how you do."

"I'd like that!" Milton said.

Over the next few weeks, Milton did his best to stay neat and tidy. At first it was difficult, but the more he did his jobs and remembered to pick up after himself and stay neat, the easier it became. Then one evening his father brought home a wagon just like the one Bumble had won. He presented it to Milton as a reward for doing his jobs faithfully and having good manners.

Milton was so happy! And you know what? From then on, Milton was always known for his good manners, faithfulness, and neatness.

"I want to do my best to be more neat and tidy, Grandpa," Tristan said.

"That's wonderful!" replied Grandpa Jake. "I'm sure it will make your mother very happy."

"I'm going to go upstairs and clean up my room. That way, when Mom comes home, she'll be so surprised to see how neat and tidy it is," exclaimed Tristan.

Bedtime Blues

It's five minutes till bedtime, Tristan," Grandpa Jake said, poking his head around the door to Tristan's room.

"Do I have to go to bed now?" Tristan asked.

"Sleep is good for you," Grandpa Jake explained. "Sleep helps you to stay healthy. It also helps you grow and have energy for the next day."

"But can't I read for a little longer?" pleaded Tristan.

"How about instead I tell you a story about Wesley, and what happened to him when he didn't get the rest he needed?"

"Okay," Tristan said, putting his book away.

"Tomorrow we are going on a nature hike," announced Mr. Nuggin.

"Hooray!" the excited students chorused.

"It's very important that everyone gets a good night's sleep before we leave," Mr. Nuggin explained. "We're going to leave early in the morning, and you'll need a lot of energy for the hike."

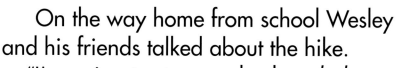

On the way home from school Wesley and his friends talked about the hike.

"I'm going to stay awake the *whole* night!" Wesley exclaimed. "That way I'll be the first one ready."

"That's a silly idea," said Suds.

"If you don't sleep tonight, you'll be very tired tomorrow," said Crispin. "No, I won't," answered Wesley. "I'll show you."

That night when all the other dinosaurs went to sleep, Wesley did his best to stay awake. He read for as long as he possibly could. He crept around the den when his family was asleep. He also got himself some food to snack on. Wesley told himself stories. He even tried to count *all* the stars in the sky, though he always seemed to lose count and would have to start again.

I'll show Suds and Crispin that I can stay up all night, Wesley told himself. *I'll be just fine, and more ready for the hike than they are!*

As the sun crept over the horizon, Wesley jumped out of bed and hurried to get his stuff together.

"Good morning, Wesley," his mother said. "You're up bright and early. Did you sleep well?"

"I didn't…," Wesley began. "I mean … just fine, thank you."

"From what Mr. Nuggin told your father and me, your hike today is going to be quite a big one," his mother said. "So it's good you're rested."

"I'm ready before you guys," Wesley boasted when he saw his friends. "And I stayed up *all* night long!"

"You're going to get tired," Suds said.

"I don't think so!" replied Wesley.

When the group of hikers had gathered, Mr. Nuggin set a few rules and then said a prayer for their safekeeping. They were ready to set off.

At first, Wesley was right at the front of the group of hikers. However, as the morning wore on, Wesley started to fall to the back of the group. The mountain path got steeper and steeper, and Wesley was often yawning and out of breath.

"Is something wrong?" Suds asked Wesley, when she saw him lagging behind the group. "Are you tired?"

"Not at all!" Wesley lied. "If I stay behind everyone, I can see the trees better, and I can catch things everyone else misses."

"I'm so glad I slept well last night, because I have lots of energy for this trip," Suds said.

Wesley didn't answer. With each step, his legs felt heavier and heavier. The higher they climbed, the colder Wesley felt. He put on both his sweaters, but he still couldn't get warm.

"Where's Wesley?" Mr. Nuggin asked a short while later. Everyone looked back down the path; Wesley was nowhere to be seen.

"We'd better find him," Mr. Nuggin said. "I hope he's not lost!"

After several minutes of searching, they found Wesley curled up at the base of a large tree. He was shivering, and his eyes were tired and droopy.

"Are you okay, Wesley?" Mr. Nuggin asked.

Wesley's bottom lip quivered, and he yawned. When Wesley tried to stand, his legs were shaky. He was completely exhausted and couldn't hike any further.

"Oh dear, it looks like we're going to have to head back home," Mr. Nuggin said.

"But Mr. Nuggin, we haven't made it to the top yet," Crispin said.

"I know. But I don't think Wesley will be able to make it any further. We'll have to head back, and perhaps try this climb again another time."

The group of hikers sadly turned back down the mountain and made their way home. Wesley had to ride on Mr. Nuggin's back, as he was too weak to walk.

For several days Wesley was sick in bed. He had caught a nasty cold because he was tired, run-down, and chilled.

"I think Crispin and Suds are upset at me," Wesley told his mother one evening, when she came to check in on him.

"Why is that?" his mother asked.

"Because I ruined the hike. You see, I … I lied when I said I slept well the night before our hike. I actually stayed up all night. I thought that I'd be more ready for the hike."

"Well, that explains why you got so tired and sick," his mother said. "Your body didn't have the energy for the hike, or even to keep you warm, so you got chilled."

"I'm so sorry," Wesley said with tears in his eyes. "If I had known this was going to happen, I wouldn't have stayed up all night. Instead, I would've gone to sleep."

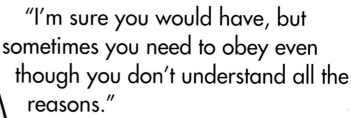

"I'm sure you would have, but sometimes you need to obey even though you don't understand all the reasons."

After Wesley was better, he returned to school. Wesley asked Mr. Nuggin if he could say something to the rest of the class.

"I'm very sorry that everyone had to stop the hike early because of me," Wesley began. "The truth is that I had decided not to sleep the night before our hike, because I thought I'd be more ready if I didn't sleep. But I was wrong. I ended up getting sick, and no one was able to make it to the top of the mountain. I'm also sorry for not telling the truth."

"Thank you, Wesley, for explaining your lesson to the class," Mr. Nuggin said. "We forgive you, and I'm sure it's a lesson that everyone can learn from, too."

A couple of weeks later, Mr. Nuggin said they were going to try to climb the mountain again, and reminded everyone to have a good night's sleep.

Wesley went home, and asked his parents if he could go to bed earlier than normal. He wanted to be fit and ready for

the hike. The next day Wesley was full of energy, and wasn't tired at all. The group made it to the top of the mountain and back without any problems.

"If I was going to go on a hike, I'd be sure to sleep super well the night before," Tristan said.

"I'm happy to hear that," said Grandpa Jake. "But you know, it's important that you are faithful to get good rest *all* the time."

"Why?"

"Your body is strengthened when you sleep," Grandpa Jake explained. "Sleep gives you energy for the next day. If you don't get enough sleep, then your body gets weaker. When your body is weaker, you're more likely to get sick."

"I don't like to be sick," Tristan said. "So I'd better rest and go to sleep."

"That's right."

Moral:

Your body needs proper care in order to stay healthy. If you sleep well and eat well, you will be less likely to get sick.

Suds, Soap, and Shells

It was Tristan's birthday, and his parents had given him a pop-up tent as a present. Tristan was eager to camp out in it. Grandpa Jake suggested that Tristan invite some of his friends over, so they could camp in the back yard. Tristan was very excited and invited Troy, Chantal, and Derek over.

Soon Tristan's friends arrived, bringing an extra tent, their sleeping bags, flashlights, snacks, and some books to read. They all worked together with Grandpa Jake to set the tents up.

Troy had noticed a large flashlight that Chantal had brought with her. He thought her flashlight was a lot nicer than his, and he wanted to see how well it worked. He turned it on and off a couple of times, but because it was still light outside, he couldn't see how bright the flashlight was.

Hmmm … I know! Troy thought to himself. *It'll be darker inside the sleeping bag.*

Troy climbed into Chantal's sleeping bag and switched the flashlight on and off, on and off.

Chantal had been playing outside, and then she walked towards the tent and saw a light going on and off inside her sleeping bag. "What are you doing in my sleeping bag?" she asked Troy angrily.

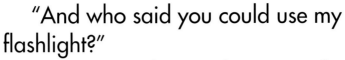

"And who said you could use my flashlight?"

"I-I just wanted to see how your flashlight worked," Troy answered.

Chantal angrily reached out to grab the flashlight, and noticed the light slowly fading. The flashlight batteries had died!

Chantal burst into tears. "I'm going to take your batteries now," she said to Troy.

She leaned over to get Troy's flashlight, but he was quicker than she was. He took his flashlight and ran away quickly.

Chantal went to Grandpa Jake and told him what Troy had done.

"I'm sorry your batteries are dead, and I'm sad about what Troy did, as it wasn't right," Grandpa Jake said. "But there are better ways to solve problems than getting angry. It's important that you work things out in love.

"Why don't I tell you a story about Suds and Dixie, and what happened when they got into a similar situation?"

Dixie loved to paint. Her favorite things to paint were flowers and butterflies, because she could make them bright and colorful! Dixie didn't only paint on paper; she would also

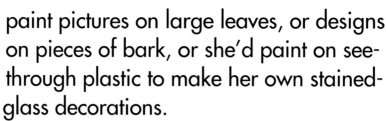

paint pictures on large leaves, or designs on pieces of bark, or she'd paint on see-through plastic to make her own stained-glass decorations.

Mr. Nuggin had asked his students to bring to class something they had personally made. Dixie brought some of her favorite paintings, Suds brought colored soap bars, and Wesley brought a matchstick house. Each student took turns presenting his or her artistic creations.

As Dixie was leaving school, she saw Suds' soap bars. Suddenly, Dixie had an idea. *I could paint pictures on a soap bar and decorate it for my mother!*

When no one was looking, Dixie took one of the soap bars—without asking Suds..

"You *stole* my soap bar, Dixie!" Suds cried out, when she saw Dixie painting and decorating the soap.

Dixie hadn't realized that Suds had come to visit her, and was surprised to see Suds standing next to her. She quickly tried to hide the soap bar.

"You're the one who took my soap bar! And now you're messing it all up."

"I'm not messing it up. I'm decorating it."

"Give it back to me," Suds said.

Dixie shook her head. "I've worked hard to decorate and paint it, and I'm going to give it to my mother as a gift."

Suds was very upset. Then she saw a bag of shells that Dixie had been collecting. When Dixie wasn't looking, Suds grabbed the bag of shells and quickly left Dixie's den.

I'd better hide these shells, Suds thought as she hurried home, stuffing the bag in her pocket.

When she got back to her den, Suds went to her room to find a place to hide Dixie's shells. Suddenly she heard her mother's voice! Quickly she put the bag under her bedcover, but the shells made the bedcover look lumpy, so just before her mother came into the room Suds sat on the shells.

But as she did, she realized she had made a terrible mistake.

Crunch! Crunch!

"Have you seen your brother?" her mother asked.

Suds shook her head quickly.

"Well, if you do see him, tell him he needs to finish his homework."

When her mother left, Suds carefully looked into the bag and saw that several of the shells were broken. *Oh dear! What am I going to do?* she thought. *Dixie is going to be so angry at me.*

But then Suds thought, *Dixie did take my soap without asking, so it serves her right that her shells got broken.*

A few hours went by. The more Suds thought about the shells, the worse she felt. "Maybe I should tell Dixie," she would say to herself. But each time she would decide against it.

That night when her mother came to tuck her in, Suds was feeling very sad.

"What's wrong, sweetheart?" her mother asked.

Suds told her mother what had happened with Dixie's shells. "I don't know what to do," Suds said with a sob.

"It's always best to be honest," her mother answered. "Dixie will probably be sad, but it's better that you tell her.

You were upset that Dixie took your soap, but you shouldn't have taken her shells, because that got you into a mess."

Suds gave her mother a hug. "I'll tell Dixie about her shells tomorrow."

"Dixie, yesterday I took your shells from your room when you weren't looking," Suds began. "I was so angry at you for taking my soap that I wanted to make you feel bad, too."

"You took my shells?" Dixie asked angrily, grabbing the bag of shells Suds was holding out to her.

"Yes, and I'm so sorry that I accidentally broke some of them."

Dixie looked into her bag of shells and cried when she saw that some of her shells were broken. "Oh, Suds, some of these were my favorite shells," she said.

"I'm so sorry," Suds replied.

Dixie thought for a moment. "I'm the one who should be sorry," she said. "I should have asked before taking your soap, and not only thought about myself and what I wanted."

"I forgive you," said Suds. "You can keep the soap bar, and I have another one for you too if you want."

"Thank you so much. I have an idea of what we can do with these broken shells. We can decorate a box by gluing the broken shells to the outside of the box. It can be our friendship box."

The two friends hugged, and happily set out to find the necessary items to make their friendship box.

"I'm sorry for wasting your batteries," Troy said to Chantal. "You can use my flashlight if you'd like."

"I forgive you," Chantal said. "And I'm sorry for getting angry at you."

"Well, that's much better," Grandpa Jake said. "You know, I think I might have an extra set of batteries that you can use, Chantal."

"Really?"

"Yes. Make sure that you use your flashlight only when you need to, and then your batteries will last much longer."

"Thank you, Grandpa Jake, for helping us work this out," Chantal said.

"And thank you for the story," Troy added.

Moral: Think about how the things you do will make other people feel, and treat others as you'd like them to treat you. If you make others happy, you will be happy too.

Manners Manor

It was dinnertime, and with his fork and spoon Tristan had built a small hill out of his mashed potatoes. He took two peas and held them at the top of the hill. "On your marks, get set … go!" he said, then rolled the peas down the miniature mashed potato hill, to see which would reach the bottom first.

"Tristan, this is my last warning," his mother said. "It's not good manners to play with your food."

Tristan had been at the table for quite some time already, playing with his food. Everyone else had already finished and left the table. Around Tristan's plate were many pieces of food that had fallen or been knocked off, and his hands were messy and sticky.

Grandpa Jake walked in.

"My, my. Tristan, it's almost your bedtime, and who would've thought you'd still be here eating?"

"I'm having a hard time with my dinner, Grandpa," Tristan said. "Eating takes *so* long."

"Well, you'll find it takes a lot longer to eat when you're playing with your food. If you have good manners and don't play with your food, then eating doesn't take that long. Did you ever hear of Manners Manor, Tristan?"

"No," answered Tristan.

"That might be just the perfect story for now," Grandpa Jake said thoughtfully.

"But you'll need to eat up before I can tell you the story."

Tristan sat straight up and removed his elbows from the table, scooped up some mashed potatoes and peas and took a large bite.

"Excellent!" exclaimed Grandpa Jake. "If you take bites like that, you'll be done in no time. Let's see now … Manners Manor."

Bumble had a difficult time sitting still at mealtimes and eating nicely. No matter how often her mother insisted that she sit still and eat properly, Bumble seemed to forget, and instead wiggled about in her chair, leaning on her elbows and chewing with her mouth open. She'd get up from the table without being excused, and when the meal was something she didn't really like, she would take a very long time to eat it. At almost every meal, it seemed that Bumble left a big mess all over the table, her clothes, and on the floor.

Her mother would often remind her of the importance of having good manners. Bumble would apologize, but by the next meal she had forgotten what her mother had said.

One evening before dinner, Bumble's mother announced that she had something special for her, and handed her an envelope. Bumble opened it and pulled out a beautifully written invitation:

Dear Lady Bumble,

It would be our greatest pleasure to invite you to Manners Manor for this year's banquet. It will be held two weeks from today, starting at 4 o'clock in the afternoon. We look forward to seeing you.

Sincerely,
Lord and Lady Manners

"Who are Lord and Lady Manners, Mom?" Bumble asked.

"They're friends of ours," Bumble's mother said, "who you'll meet at the banquet. It's a special occasion, and those who attend have only the best table manners."

"Then maybe I shouldn't go," Bumble said with a sigh. "I don't have very good manners."

"This is a wonderful chance to learn! You have two weeks before the banquet to work on your manners."

Bumble brightened up. Together they made a list of manners that Bumble could improve in.

Bumble was so eager to be a good example of being polite and having good table manners, that she made an extra effort at every meal. Soon Bumble began to enjoy her mealtimes more. By the time of the banquet, Bumble was ready.

"Good evening, Lady Bumble," the butler said as he greeted her at the door of the manor. "It's a pleasure to have you here tonight."

"It's nice to be here," Bumble replied.

Bumble looked around the room, and noticed that many of her friends were there too. She saw Dixie and Suds across the room and was about to call out to them when she remembered. *Oops, I shouldn't call out like that! Mother told me that it's not polite to shout in company like this.*

Bumble walked over to her friends. Each one explained about the invitation and how they had worked on their manners. "Do you know who Lord and Lady Manners are?" Milton asked the others.

"My mother said they're friends," Bumble replied.

No one else seemed to know anything else about Lord and Lady Manners, but all were excited about meeting them.

Suddenly there was a brief chime of a bell, and the butler announced that dinner would begin. They entered the dining room and saw a long table, well laden with food. Each place at the table was set with special care, with a different plate, napkin, and silverware set. There was a name card by each plate.

Bumble saw her name card and was about to sit down, when she noticed that the plate, napkin, and silverware at Dixie's place were in her favorite color.

"I want to sit where you're sitting!" Bumble demanded.

"But this is my seat," Dixie replied. "My name card is here."

Bumble grabbed Dixie's name card and switched it with hers.

"Don't be mean. This is where *I'm* meant to sit, and that's where *you're* meant to sit."

But Bumble wanted to sit in Dixie's place. Just as Dixie was about to sit down in her chair, Bumble pulled the chair out from under her. Dixie hit the floor with a thump. "Ouch!" she cried. The whole room went silent and everyone turned to look at Bumble.

Oh dear! Everyone is looking at me, Bumble thought. She felt bad.

"Dixie, I'm sorry," she said, apologizing. "We're here because we've learned to be polite, courteous and well mannered. And what I just did wasn't good manners at all."

"That's okay," Dixie said. "I forgive you."

Just then Lord and Lady Manners entered the room, and took their place at the head of the table.

"Welcome, dear friends!" Lord Manners announced. "We're so happy that you could join us. This special dinner is in recognition of your efforts to have good manners."

"Courtesy, being polite, and good manners are important habits to learn," Lady Manners added. "And we are happy to share this evening with you."

The meal began, with everyone using their very best manners ever.

"Don't Lord and Lady Manners look familiar?" Wesley asked Bumble. "In fact, I think Lord Manners looks a lot like Mr. Nuggin."

Bumble looked over at Lord and Lady Manners. Lord Manners caught her eye and winked. It *was* Mr. Nuggin and his wife.

The next morning at school, Mr. Nuggin entered the classroom whistling his favorite song.

"Good morning, Lord Manners," the students chorused happily.

"Aha, I see you've found out!" Mr. Nuggin replied with a chuckle. "Did you all enjoy yourselves last night?"

"Yes, we did!" the students answered.

"Are you really a lord, Mr. Nuggin?" Bumble asked.

"Well, not really," said Mr. Nuggin. "But because I knew how hard each of you has been working on learning better manners, I wanted to do something special for you. So, with the help of your parents, my wife and I planned last night's banquet."

"It was a wonderful idea, Mr. Nuggin! Thank you so much!" Dixie exclaimed.

"That was a lot of fun," Tristan said, as the story ended. "Maybe we can have a pretend Manners Manor like they did, and invite all my friends."

"That's a wonderful idea!" Grandpa Jake said.

Moral:

When you have good manners, it makes others happy, because it shows them love and respect.

The Christmas Chest

It was the first day of December. The afternoon was cold, and snow fell softly outside. Tristan and Derek were busy putting together a Christmas calendar. It was a picture of a manger scene, with little flaps for each day of December, and underneath each of the flaps was written a little activity or project.

Parts of the calendar were a little tricky to put together, and Derek tried to get it to work. Tristan watched impatiently. "Let me do it," he said. Then a few minutes later, again, "Let me do it!" And on it went. But each time, Derek would shake his head and keep trying.

Tristan finally got angry. "You're not doing it properly!" he said. "It's *my* calendar, and you need to give it to me, now!"

"But I'm working on it," Derek answered.

"It doesn't matter. I want it now! I shouldn't have invited you to help me."

The argument took off from there, the two boys getting angrier and angrier. Soon they were shouting and saying nasty things to each other.

"Boys, that's enough!" Grandpa Jake said, entering the room. "I was listening to you argue as I came down the hall, and you need to try and work things out nicely. Arguing doesn't

solve the problem, and just makes you more upset with each other."

Tristan and Derek looked at each other sadly.

"Did I tell you the story about the Christmas chest?" Grandpa Jake asked.

Both boys' faces brightened. "No," they chorused. "Can you tell us?"

"Yes. I think it might just help you."

Every Christmas, Dixie and Crispin's mother would pull out their family's Christmas chest. The Christmas chest was a large box with a lid, in which their mother would gather different items she found throughout the year. Dixie and Crispin could then use these items in their Christmas projects and decorations. This year, the box was exceptionally full with lots of interesting bits and pieces.

Crispin and Dixie had invited their friends over, and each one gathered around as Crispin lifted the lid off. Dixie reached in and pulled out a colorful piece of ribbon.

"It's so pretty," Suds said.

Soon all the friends were sorting through the items looking for stuff, and talking about what they'd make with the different items.

"Look what I found!" Wesley said, spotting a large shell.

"I found it first!" Milton said, and swooped up the shell.

"Oh no, you didn't," Wesley replied, trying to grab it away from Milton.

Before long the others were also quarreling among themselves, each wanting what the other one had.

"This is *my* Christmas chest," Crispin said, "and if you take the things I want, then you can't be here."

"It's my Christmas chest too," Dixie said. "It's both of ours."

"That's not fair," Wesley said.

"You're being very mean," Milton said.

And on the arguing went.

"Everybody, stop!" Suds said in a loud voice.

Everyone stopped what they were doing and looked at her.

"Christmas is a time when we're all supposed to be extra loving and kind to each other," Suds said.

"Suds is right," Milton said. "I'm sorry for taking the shell away from you, Wesley. You can have it back."

"I'm sorry too," said Wesley.

"Me too," said the others.

"I have an idea," said Suds. "We could work together to use all the things in the chest to do nice things for other people."

"We could use some of the stuff to decorate our classroom as a surprise for everyone," Wesley suggested.

"And make a wreath for Mr. Nuggin," said Bumble.

"We could also help decorate the village Christmas tree," Crispin said.

"We could make presents for our friends," Dixie added.

"Then we could use the wagons that Bumble and I have to take the gifts to everyone," Milton said.

"These are all wonderful ideas," Suds said, "and if we work on them together, we won't be worried about who gets what."

Suds got a pen and paper, and together they decided who they would make gifts for.

They decided that Crispin and Bumble would make the wreath for Mr. Nuggin, while Dixie and Wesley decorated the classroom. Milton and Suds teamed up to help decorate the village Christmas tree. If they were done with that and still had time, they would decide who else to make gifts for.

"We can use this string of lights for the classroom," Wesley said.

"Oh, but we were planning on using it for Mr. Nuggin's wreath," Crispin said, and reached over to take the lights.

"But they're too long for the wreath," Dixie added, "and they'd look much nicer in the classroom."

"Dixie…!" Crispin exclaimed, feeling a little angry. Then he stopped for a moment. "Oh dear, I almost got angry at you again, but that's not good. Why don't you take them? They really are too long for the wreath, and we can use something else instead."

"Thank you, Crispin," said Dixie. "You can have these little bells for the wreath instead."

"They're perfect!" Crispin said. "And they'll look much better on the wreath than the lights would have."

Over the weeks leading up to Christmas, the friends busied themselves in their free time, making gifts and decorations for their family and friends.

They happily worked on their projects until they had completed all of them. They had used up all the bits and pieces in the Christmas chest.

The presents were loaded up on Bumble and Milton's wagon and distributed to their friends and family. Everyone was so happy, and it was

by far the happiest Christmas the friends had shared, because they had all thought about others instead of themselves.

"Grandpa, why do people always say that Christmas is about giving?" Tristan asked.

"Aha! Good question," said Grandpa Jake. "That's because God gave us a very special gift many, many Christmases ago. Do you know what it was?"

Tristan thought for a moment, and then his face lit up. "Jesus!"

"That's right. God sent Jesus to Earth for each one of us. He was God's Christmas present to each one of us. And when we have Jesus in our lives, we are so much happier, and our lives are filled with more joy!"

"But why do we give presents?"

"When we give things to other people, it makes them happy and it shows them that we love and think about them."

"I like to make people happy by doing nice things for them," Tristan said.

"Thank you for telling us that story, Grandpa! It was a wonderful Christmas story."

"My pleasure," answered Grandpa Jake.

Morals highlighted in
Dino Tales

In an animated and fun format, each story in Dino Tales focuses on one of these character-building morals:

- Everyone makes mistakes, and needs forgiveness. Forgiveness is love. (From "Operation Oops!")

- When people see that you are responsible, they are more likely to trust you with things, because they know you'll take good care of them. (From "My Oh My, Milton!")

- Your body needs proper care in order to stay healthy. If you sleep well and eat well, you will be less likely to get sick. (From "Bedtime Blues")

- Think about how the things you do will make other people feel, and treat others as you'd like them to treat you. If you make others happy, you will be happy too. (From "Suds, Soap, and Shells")

- When you have good manners, it makes others happy, because it shows them love and respect. (From "Manners Manor")

- Show kindness to others, and take time to work out your differences with love, and you'll get along well with others, and everyone will be happy. (From "The Christmas Chest")

GRANDPA JAKE'S STORYBOOK

Crew and Co.

Come along with a team of hard-working construction vehicles including Dee the Dump truck, Lorry Loader, Crank Crane, the Con Crete Brothers and cheery Digger. Working together under wise Mr. Oversite, they each play an important part in completing the crew and getting the job done.

- ✓ Seeing a job through
- ✓ Following instructions
- ✓ Doing the right thing
- ✓ Resolving arguments
- ✓ Helping others
- ✓ Working as a team

Dino Tales

A group of dinosaur friends live a happy life together, filled with adventure and opportunities to show their concern for one another. When Crispin accidentally ruins his sister Dixie's garden, they and their friends work together to repair what's been damaged. Wesley's bedtime blues turn into a misadventure, but one with lessons worth having learned. A surprise invitation presents Bumble with the challenge of brushing up on manners fit for a banquet.

- ✓ Thinking about others
- ✓ Courtesy
- ✓ Healthy habits
- ✓ Obedience
- ✓ Honesty
- ✓ Resolving conflict
- ✓ Forgiveness